Book 1

Copyrights

Just for Today Book 1

First Edition 2017

ISBN : 978-1979224260

About this book ...

'Just for Today' is the phrase that seeds the nuggets of mindfulness that have been dropping into peoples' In Boxes for just over two years now. The aim is to light up the world by changing thoughts, deeds and actions one person at a time. They come from the pen of author and meditation guide, Tom Evans.

In the middle of this year, an amazing artist, called Siri Stiklestad Opli, approached Tom and asked him if he would like them to be illustrated. Tom had been waiting for a Siri to arrive. This book is the first of many collections of their co-creations.

Each of the 75 nuggets of mindfulness in this book encourages you to capture your thoughts, either in words or sketches, and to take action as a result. So this is not so much a workbook but a 'Thoughts & Actions' book.

Note that slowing down is the new speeding up and this is also one book where reading, absorbing and acting on a page a day has special benefits.

Pay close attention to the gaps between the words and the white space in and around the illustrations, as that's where the magic lies.

♡ THOUGHTS & ACTIONS ♡

Just for today, Tom, bewitch and beguile.

The best magic tricks are those where nobody actually notices that any magic has been done. Being alive on Planet Earth is a great example of this - we just take it for granted.

So, without announcing or declaring it, use your magical gifts to make a change in someone's world. Be mindful though that they shouldn't be aware magic is in operation - but just notice the end result.

♡ THOUGHTS & ACTIONS ♡

Just for today, soften your stance.

Desist resisting.

Stop protesting.

And allow.

♡ THOUGHTS & ACTIONS ♡

Just for today, be in awe of the cosmos.

What forces have been brought to bear to create the planet we call home?

What stars have died so you can live?

What art and science has allowed this book to be published and read?

♡ THOUGHTS & ACTIONS ♡

Just for today, big someone up.

Make someone a celebrity for a day.
Share why they have made a difference in your world.
Make known to the world, someone who may be un-known.

♡ THOUGHTS & ACTIONS ♡

Just for today, stand up and be counted.

Rally around a cause or a friend with a cause.
Take the load off someone's shoulders for someone else
who needs some respite.

♡ THOUGHTS & ACTIONS ♡

Just for today, notice the humangels.

We are surrounded by human-angels.

Most of them don't know what they are.

The ones that do, take care not to be noticed.

♡ THOUGHTS & ACTIONS ♡

Just for today, ask for help.

Make a list of things you could do with help with and just park it somewhere.
If anyone comes along, and asks "Is there anything I can help you with?",
let them step in.
This way your To Do list, and how it gets done, is handed over to
the Universe to actually do !!

♡ THOUGHTS & ACTIONS ♡

Just for today, develop your 'blissipline'.

Cultivate happiness by sprinkling seeds of joy on your path.

Perform small random acts of kindness as you go about your day.

Treat yourself often & be guilt-free.

♡ THOUGHTS & ACTIONS ♡

Just for today, let it pour.

Turn your creativity into a torrent.

Just let your creativity flow easily and speedily.

Be gushing in all you do today.

♡ THOUGHTS & ACTIONS ♡

Just for today, introspect.

Close your doors, windows and shutters to the outside world.

Contemplate your thoughts.

Who is actually talking in your head and who is doing the listening?

♡ THOUGHTS & ACTIONS ♡

Just for today, love what you loathe.

Think about what gets your goat and makes your blood boil.

Why does it ire you exactly?

How could you evolve by rising above it?

Then look back at your e-motions as energy pointing in the wrong direction.

♡ THOUGHTS & ACTIONS ♡

Just for today, help unexpectedly.

If you see someone in need, rush to their aid.

If you need help, ask the Universe for assistance.

At all times deliver and accept assistance when it is least expected.

♡ THOUGHTS & ACTIONS ♡

Just for today, just breathe.

Specifically, do this when you switch from one task to another by putting your
hands on your belly so your middle fingers just touch.
Breathe in so your belly swells and your fingers part.
Then breathe out around four times as long as the in breath
so that the fingers touch again.
Repeat either 3, 5, 7 or 9 times.
In and out ...

♡ THOUGHTS & ACTIONS ♡

Just for today, walk the difficult path.

Sometimes what we fear the most refuses to go away until we face it off.

Be brave and do the thing that you know you must do.

The path is clear on the other side and true abundance awaits you.

Go for it !

♡ THOUGHTS & ACTIONS ♡

Just for today, be brief.

Only use what words are necessary.
This applies to talking 'out loud' and 'in loud'.
Take the shortest route to the desired end result.

♡ THOUGHTS & ACTIONS ♡

Just for today, think back to your youth.

What did you do when you were younger that you were most proud of?

What difference did it make it the world back then?

What difference has it made to form the person you are now?

♡ THOUGHTS & ACTIONS ♡

Just for today, spot what is lurking.

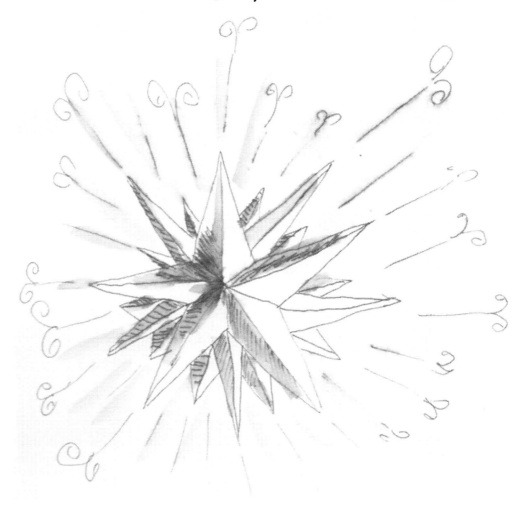

Something remarkable lurks for us around every corner.
What is about to burst into your world right now?
What can you do to bring it closer and let it in?

♡ THOUGHTS & ACTIONS ♡

Just for today, be magnetic.

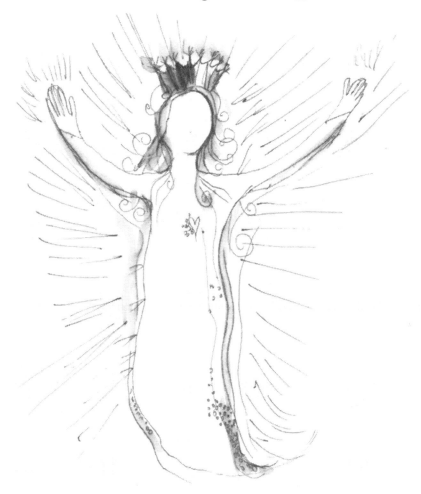

Imagine you are the North Pole of a magnet.

Imagine that those you seek to help are South Poles.

Remember magnetic force works under the Square Law.

Double your attractiveness and you become four times more attractive.

♡ THOUGHTS & ACTIONS ♡

Just for today, maintain your equilibrium.

Keep excitement to a minimum.
Keep wobbles low.
If it's 'windy out there', keep your head down and stay indoors.

♡ THOUGHTS & ACTIONS ♡

Just for today, re-treat yourself.

A retreat is a step or more backwards.
Sprinkle in a hyphen.
You will find a re-treat takes you forward.
Take one today.

♡ THOUGHTS & ACTIONS ♡

Just for today, apply

When you have to act, check in with your heart and gut.

Allow them to inform your brain as to what is right and proper to do.

Repeat daily !

THOUGHTS & ACTIONS ♡

Just for today, count your blessings.

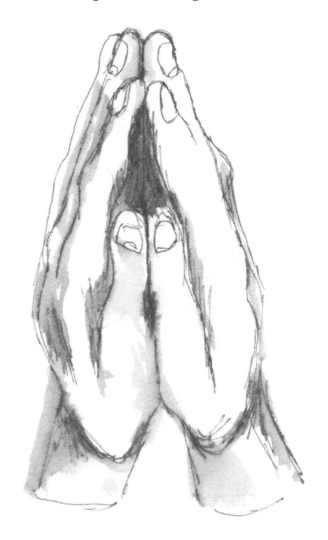

What are you thank-full for?
What do you possess that money can't buy?
Now go for a re-count.

♡ THOUGHTS & ACTIONS ♡

Just for today, ease your heart.

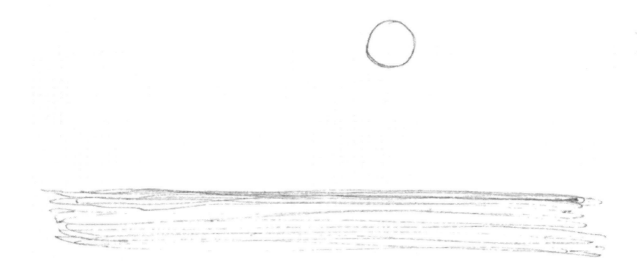

Give peace of mind to yourself and others.
Tell them that when they are calm, the waves in the ocean will calm.
Tread water with minimal effort today and make a big splash tomorrow.

♡ THOUGHTS & ACTIONS ♡

Just for today, talk to yourself.

Ask your future self what you have to do in order to evolve into
the most perfect version of you.
Take heed of the answers - and note that they might come in surprising forms.

♡ THOUGHTS & ACTIONS ♡

Just for today, dress down.

Remove all veneers and allow your true colours to show.
Wear what you like.
Do what you like.
Eat what you fancy.

♡ THOUGHTS & ACTIONS ♡

Just for today, apply some polish.

Buff up what's lacklustre in your world and make it shine.
Remove the dust from an unused possession, or talent,
and share it with the world.

♡ THOUGHTS & ACTIONS ♡

Just for today, be spirit-full.

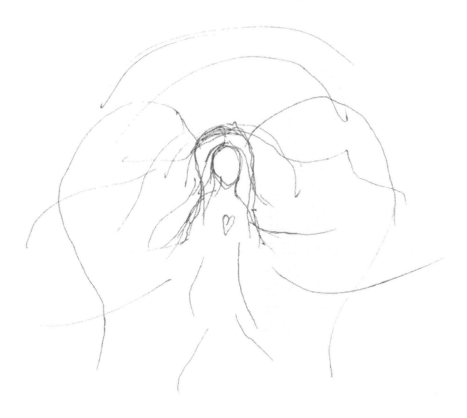

We are three dimensional projections of multi-dimensional beings.
Our physical body is like the tip of an iceberg floating in
the collective sea of consciousness.
Lighten your physical density so that more of the hidden you
pokes about the surface.
Notice how others take heed and follow in your steps.

♡ THOUGHTS & ACTIONS ♡

Just for today, start a rumour.

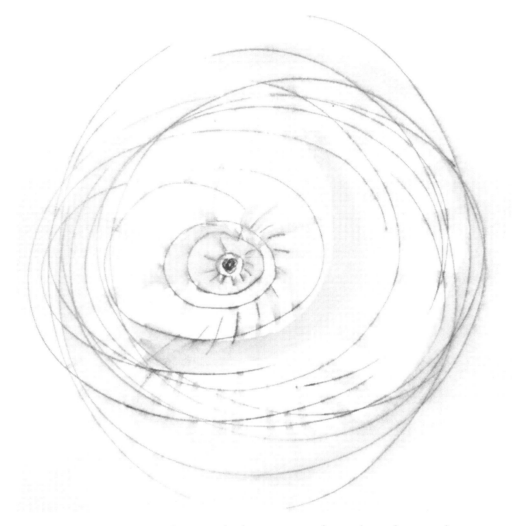

Make sure it's not mere tittle-tattle but something big that's about to unfold.
Ask for help in areas where the idea needs more substance.
Dispel the notion that life is intrinsically tough.

♡ THOUGHTS & ACTIONS ♡

Just for today, be gentle.

Be gentle on yourself.
Be gentle with others.
Tread lightly.

♡ THOUGHTS & ACTIONS ♡

Just for today, ring your bells.

Call your friends and family to join you for a celebration.
No excuses or special occasion needed.
Just being alive is cause enough.

♡ THOUGHTS & ACTIONS ♡

Just for today, remember that all is illusion.

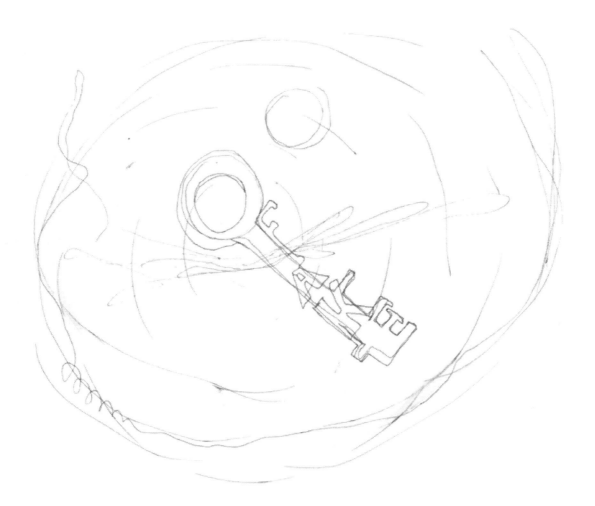

Our brains merely interpret what is out there.
The thing about this illusion is that we can all see through it.
Daily meditation is the key that unlocks that door.

♡ THOUGHTS & ACTIONS ♡

Just for today, be a busy body.

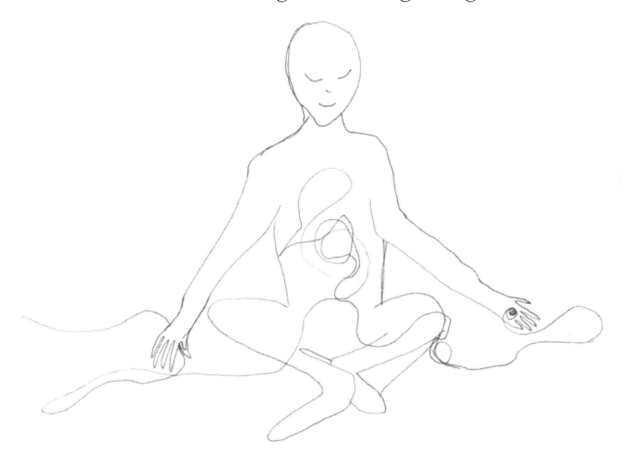

Do this by not poking your nose in the affairs of others.
Fully engage yourself in tasks and projects of your own.
Complete what is incomplete and repeat daily.

♡ THOUGHTS & ACTIONS ♡

Just for today, call others to action.

Raise your banner high and declare your intentions to the world.
Ask for assistance where needed.
Give assistance to others with their clarion calls.

♡ THOUGHTS & ACTIONS ♡

Just for today, do something silly.

The road to enlightenment doesn't need us to be worthy, or to suffer.
Have some fun today and surprise yourself and others with your actions.
The sillier, the better.

♡ THOUGHTS & ACTIONS ♡

Just for today, go back to basics.

Re-learn something you have already learned.
Un-complicate what is complex.
Simplify where possible.

♡ THOUGHTS & ACTIONS ♡

Just for today, forgive all peccadilloes.

If anything trifling has been bugging you, let it go.
If you've been hanging on to a grievance, let it go.
Notice what space this frees up for you.

♡ THOUGHTS & ACTIONS ♡

Just for today, seek out perfection.

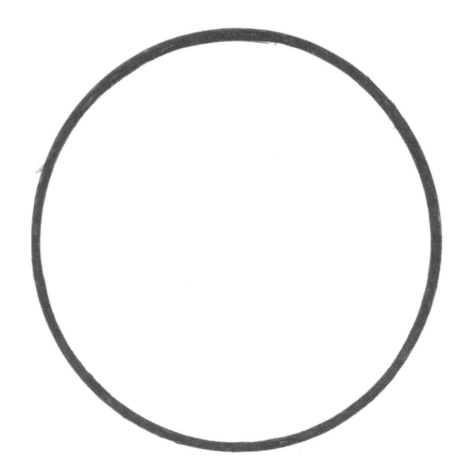

Take time to complete completely.
Smooth the edges and add a veneer to your work.
Polish it up, make it shiny and let others admire it.

♡ THOUGHTS & ACTIONS ♡

Just for today, go mythical.

Create a new story line for yourself with you as a heroine,
or hero, at the centre.
Look back at all your trials and tribulations as just that.
They are lessons learned.
Make preparations for the next phase of your journey,
then go out and change the world.

♡ THOUGHTS & ACTIONS ♡

Just for today, get to the heart of the matter.

Only do what you love.
If you don't like something, take it off your To Do list or change it,
or your attitude, to it so that you love it.
Make all decisions from the heart and just let the head observe.

♡ THOUGHTS & ACTIONS ♡

Just for today, abandon all pretences.

Who are you trying to kid?
Who says you're not worth it?
Go out and prove them wrong.

♡ THOUGHTS & ACTIONS ♡

Just for today, toast your successes.

It's time to pat yourself on the back.
For starters, you managed to incarnate on one of
the best planets in the Universe.
You are one of over 7 billion souls who also pulled this trick off.
Might be worth swapping some stories and
success tips with one or two of them.

♡ THOUGHTS & ACTIONS ♡

Just for today, give generously.

Be charitable with your time and attention, rather than with money.
Remember too that charity begins at home.
Start with yourself and spread from there.

♡ THOUGHTS & ACTIONS ♡

Just for today, let something go.

Sometimes we hang on to things longer than their Use-By-Date.
If you haven't used a possession for a while, take it to a charity shop
so someone else can enjoy it.
If you've been weighed down by a problem or belief, let it fly off with the wind.

♡ THOUGHTS & ACTIONS ♡

Just for today, create a token.

Find an object you cherish and imbue it with good will and intent.
Thank it for being the vessel for your wishes.
Touch it daily and thank it when your desires come to pass.

♡ THOUGHTS & ACTIONS ♡

Just for today, say yes to everything.

Start by saying goodbye to the naysayer in you.
When opportunities arrive today, say yes to them all.
If you hear someone else saying "No", jump in with both feet.

♡ THOUGHTS & ACTIONS ♡

Just for today, flock together.

As starlings will tell you, there is safety in numbers.
Seek out Like Minds and stick with them.
Fly in formation and make nests together.

♡ THOUGHTS & ACTIONS ♡

Just for today, profit from your labours.

Be the recipient of your best endeavours.
Enjoy being rewarded for what you do.
Then re-invest some of it on yourself.

♡ THOUGHTS & ACTIONS ♡

Just for today, give some support.

As you go about your day, be watch-full for those in a place of weakness.

They may be physically or mentally frail.

Give them a hand, a shoulder or an ear.

♡ THOUGHTS & ACTIONS ♡

Just for today, be open to the light.

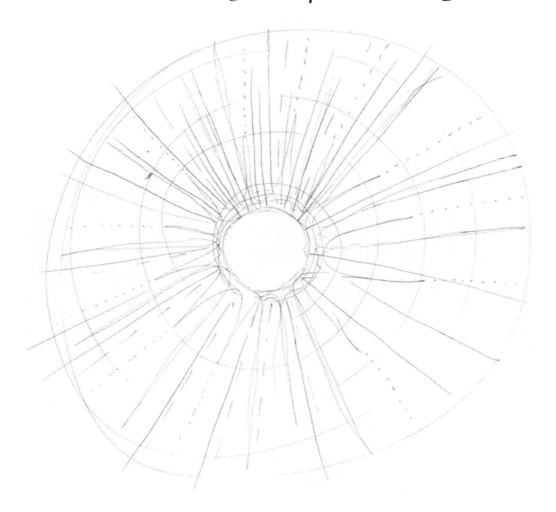

Give thanks to the Sun as the Light Giver.
Thank the trees for being the Light Batteries.
Be mindful of your true purpose as a Light Reflector.

♡ THOUGHTS & ACTIONS ♡

Just for today, show off your finery.

Put your best frock on, even if it's metaphorical, and strut your stuff.
Be thankful of complements.
Give compliments on your travels.
Be mindful of how one letter changes everything.

♡ THOUGHTS & ACTIONS ♡

Just for today, go public.

Hit the presses and tell the world what you are up to.

Come out from the shadows.

Show them what you're made of and what you've got.

♡ THOUGHTS & ACTIONS ♡

Just for today, make your own way.

Observe the paths others are taking and forge your own.
As always, leave breadcrumbs for others to follow.
Keep a journal and make a map of the new territories you find.

♡ THOUGHTS & ACTIONS ♡

Just for today, find peace and quiet.

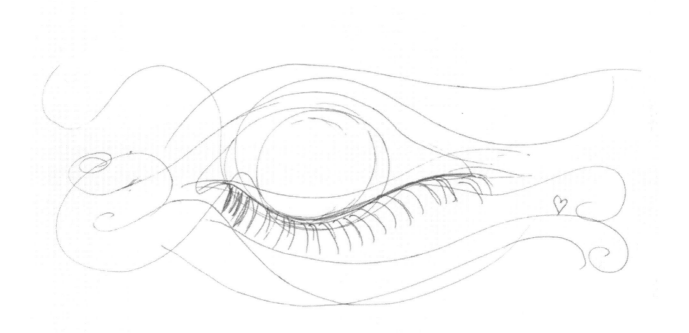

In either space, time or both, carve out at least 10 minutes all to yourself.

Put your phone into Aeroplane Mode and take a Helicopter View.

Sky rocket even higher still should you wish.

♡ THOUGHTS & ACTIONS ♡

Just for today, go sideways.

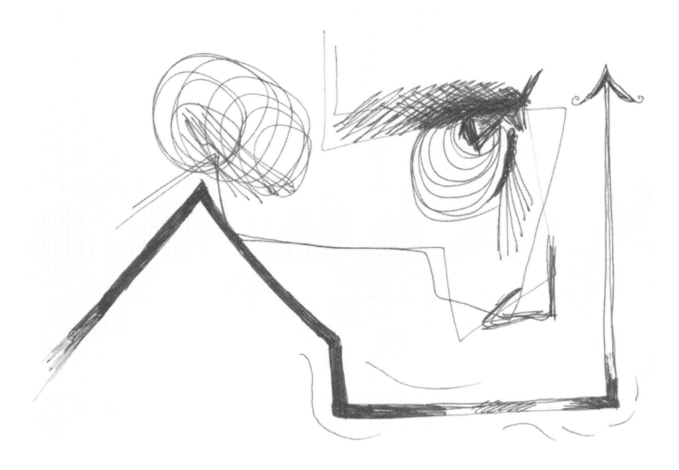

If you've felt something blocking you, take one step back,
then three steps to either the left or right.
Pause so the blockage thinks you've lost interest and
then take two steps forwards.

♡ THOUGHTS & ACTIONS ♡

Just for today, melt someone's heart.

Do something so lovely for someone, when they are not expecting it.
Make their day and you make yours too!
What goes around comes to ground.

♡ THOUGHTS & ACTIONS ♡

Just for today, do everything by the book.

Dot all the I's

Cross the T's.

Only move forward when it's perfectly right.

♡ THOUGHTS & ACTIONS ♡

Just for today, ease into the day.

Let the day come to you.
Only respond if a response is necessary.
Keep a weather-eye out though for any changes in conditions

♡ THOUGHTS & ACTIONS ♡

Just for today, give hope.

If you come across a person or situation that looks or sounds hope-less,
offer a hand of support.
Rather than dispensing the platitude that things will turn out OK,
take action to make things hope-full and full of hope.

♡ THOUGHTS & ACTIONS ♡

Just for today, declare your intentions.

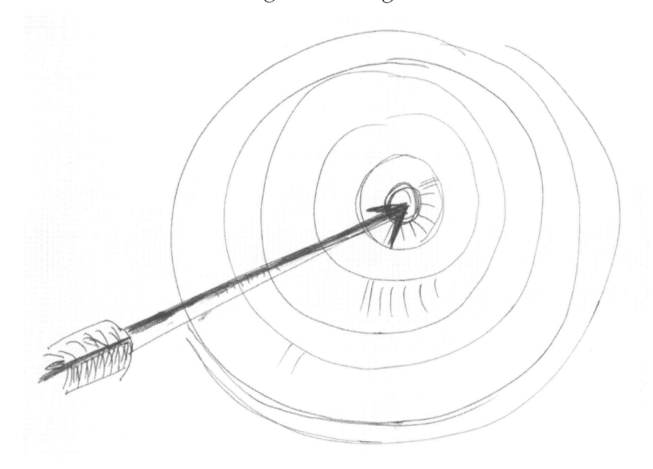

Share your goals and dreams.
Share the What, the How and, most importantly the When.
Then take one step closer to making them happen.

♡ THOUGHTS & ACTIONS ♡

Just for today, it's audit time.

Make a list of all your best attributes, skills and assets.
Add dates of when you acquired them.
Assess if any of the parts need replacing, or upgrading.

♡ THOUGHTS & ACTIONS ♡

Just for today, be talismanic.

Make your influence felt.
Draw a symbol that captures the essence of your power.
Imbue it with your intent.

♡ THOUGHTS & ACTIONS ♡

Just for today, avoid any false superiority.

Remember all hu-mans are angels-in-training, at different stages.
Being able to incarnate is an advanced skill only a few souls have pulled off.
Be prepared for any upgrades.

♡ THOUGHTS & ACTIONS ♡

Just for today, stick together.

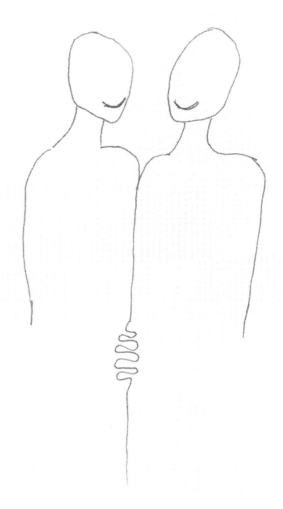

Make a call to an old friend who shares your values and vision.
Find out where they are on their Soul's Quest
and share where you are on yours.
Swap notes about what you know.

♡ THOUGHTS & ACTIONS ♡

Just for today, let people know you have arrived.

Dump false modesty.
Shout from the roof tops.
Let people know what you've done and what you are just about to do.

♡ THOUGHTS & ACTIONS ♡

Just for today, feather your nest.

Take a look around at your environment.
Observe where it's a bit tired.
Bring in some new 'furniture' and make yourself comfortable.

♡ THOUGHTS & ACTIONS ♡

Just for today, take a sabbatical.

Take a break from what ever project you are on and either go out
and have some fun or learn something new.
Come back the next day with fresh eyes and a fresh mind
and integrate an element of what you got up to.

♡ THOUGHTS & ACTIONS ♡

Just for today, be phonologically ambiguous.

Have fun with a pun and put the world to writes.
Notice how a word that sounds the same but that has a different meaning
changes a sentence – or is that a 'sent tense'?

♡ THOUGHTS & ACTIONS ♡

Just for today, seek out tranquility.

Walk away from all noise and dis-harmony.
Let that be the world for others.
Create space and time in your day to be still and to still those around you.

♡ THOUGHTS & ACTIONS ♡

Just for today, lose your shadow.

All thought forms have corresponding anti-thoughts.
Pay attention to any anti-thoughts running around your head.
Neutralise any unwanted thoughts by reframing from
the negative to the positive

♡ THOUGHTS & ACTIONS ♡

Just for today, make the unreal real.

Just imagine the un-imaginal.
Take at least one step forward into making a miracle happen.
Smile when it unfolds.

♡ THOUGHTS & ACTIONS ♡

Just for today, dine out.

Share your most wondrous stories.
If they have been heard before, give them a new slant.
Go a little deeper and share some more of the back story.

♡ THOUGHTS & ACTIONS ♡

Just for today, be illogical.

Assume all you know is wrong.
For example, the Sun never really sets, it's just a phenomenon of the Earth
rotating on its axis as it revolves around the Sun.
The Universe is not out to get you, you have just heard
that rumour somewhere and have taken it to be true.

♡ THOUGHTS & ACTIONS ♡

Just for today, be wonder-full.

Marvel at the macrocosm and microcosm.
Note how neither would exist without the other.
Let your mind fully wonder - and wander.

♡ THOUGHTS & ACTIONS ♡

Just for today, allow things to change.

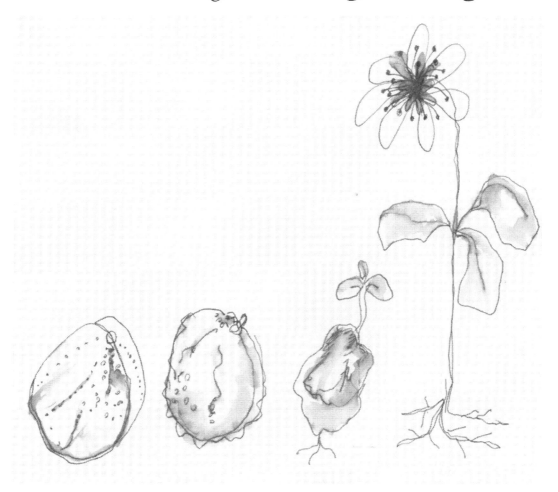

Make the un-mutable mutable.
Change resistance to acceptance.
If you find yourself being creatively uncreative, by doing everything else
but what you should be doing, stop being a Pro at Crastination.

♡ THOUGHTS & ACTIONS ♡

Just for today, go the way of a whim.

If a fancy takes you, let it do so.
Whatever you had planned today, do something else.
Let the world catch up with you when you are ready for it.

♡ THOUGHTS & ACTIONS ♡

Just for today, make the unreal real.

What is on the edge of your dreams that you would like to bring closer?
Write it down on a Post-It Note, put it under your pillow and literally sleep on it.
Then just for tomorrow, allow it to happen.

About Tom Evans

Tom is still working out what he wants to do when he wants to grows up.
He has stopped trying to plan anything as The Universe has taken control.

He once thought he was a serial entrepreneur and business man. The Universe made him into an author instead. He then wrote one book by accident and followed it with a few more - this will be the 14th!

He then thought he would be an author's mentor and the Universe convinced him otherwise. One day, unexpectedly, he discovered he'd become a meditation guide when his short meditative visualisation, entitled Just for Today, started making ripples in the pond. These nuggets of mindfulness came forth shortly after. He now knows some more iterations and surprises are on the way.

Tom currently lives in the Surrey Hills in the UK with his life partner and two labradoodles, who help him write by taking him for walks when he is stuck.
You can find out more at www.tomevans.co

About Siri Stiklestad Opli

Siri has always loved to paint and draw. Her painting style is very intuitive, and most of the times, she doesn't know what she has been painting until it is finished.

Siri loves colours, floating forms, and to paint the energy in words. To her, the spectator is the most important part of the painting. The person who looks at an image creates the motive in the now. Inspiration exists in a divine stream, which Siri only can describe as coming through her, and not from her. She is a channel for artistic expression. This is her purpose and gift to the world.

As she loves illustrating, and loves words, it is natural her gift attracts commissions from poets, bloggers and authors from all around the globe. This is what compelled her to reach out to Tom to ask if he had ever considered illustrating his nuggets of mindfulness. He hadn't but has now!

One of Siri's late teachers said, "The most creative thing you can do, in addition to painting, is to have children!" She lives in Norway with five of them.

If you have words that require imagery, connect with Siri through her web site
www.fjellbjorka.no

About Just for Today

Just for Today are free nuggets of mindfulness
gifted to your In Box each day.

The keys to living a magical and charmed life are simple. What we think, and
how we think, alters our view of the world and, as a result, the world itself.

Monday through to Friday, you will get a short email with a simple, mindful
thought for the day, along with one of Siri's beautiful illustrations.

The aim is simple. Just by making one simple change each day, we can create a
more magical world for ourselves, our family, our friends and the people
and beings who we are sharing a ride with on Spaceship Earth.

Did we mention? It's completely free!
Plus you will get an invite to connect with other 'Like-Minds'
through our Facebook group.

www.tomevans.co/justfortoday

Made in the USA
Las Vegas, NV
05 December 2020